Dear Diana,

We hope that this book
will bring back fond
memories of your stay
in the South West of
England.

With our fondest best
wishes for Christmas 1987
and for the years to come.

The Lewis Family.

The Country Life Picture Book of

Devon and Cornwall

The Country Life Picture Book of
Devon and Cornwall

Paul Pettit

COUNTRY LIFE BOOKS

Frontispiece
Knightshayes Court, Tiverton, Devon, a Victorian
mansion with 200 acres of gardens and parkland
given to the National Trust by Sir John Heathcote
Amory in 1972.

Published by Country Life Books,
an imprint of Newnes Books,
a division of The Hamlyn Publishing Group Limited,
84-88 The Centre, Feltham, Middlesex, England
and distributed for them by
The Hamlyn Publishing Group Limited
Rushden, Northants, England

First published 1982
Second impression 1985

ISBN 0 600 36822 X

Printed in Czechoslovakia
52095

Introduction

What a subject for a picture book – two of the most beautiful counties of England and, judging by the number of visitors, two of the best loved.

A traveller from London or Birmingham to Land's End is only halfway when he reaches the north-east border of Devon. Ahead lies a jagged peninsula, one hundred and forty miles in length down its spine, running out south-westwards between the Bristol and English Channels to the Atlantic. Hundreds of miles of bays, coves, estuaries, beaches and impressive cliffs and headlands culminate in two small peninsulas, Land's End thrusting west, the Lizard south. These are not dissimilar to a small version of the heel and toe of Italy and the whole region has the shape of a sloppy sea-boot. Twenty-five miles out in the Atlantic from Land's End, and separated from it by a deep and dangerous channel, lie the granite Isles of Scilly.

Naturally the coastline is the outstanding feature and few lengths of coast can bear comparison with it. The variety ranges from the warm, red cliffs of south-east Devon and the fine estuaries and natural anchorages all along the south coast to the stark walls of rock under continual assault from the Atlantic. Only St Ives Bay with its sand dunes or 'towans' and the estuaries of the rivers Camel, Taw and Torridge appear as breaches in the ramparts of the north coast. Otherwise the outfalls are mainly little rivers reaching the sea through narrow clefts, or mere streams that splash abruptly down the rocks. In contrast, the south coast seems to invite the sea to its many bays and estuaries. Between these extremes a complex geology and the clear light that has drawn so many artists to the region ensure that the eye is continually refreshed by changing shorescapes. A rugged path four hundred and fifty miles long follows the coastline, a challenging route up and down, and up and down again, sometimes as much as several hundred feet at a time.

Fortunately about a third of this coastline and the granite isle of Lundy in the Bristol Channel have been acquired over the years by the National Trust. Everyone who loves the region must hope that landowners will continue to sell or give to the Trust the undeveloped stretches not yet in its ownership.

The coasts and the comparatively short land border of Devon enclose an area of nearly four thousand square miles. Cornwall contains a little over a third of this. The population is approaching one and a half million, of which a little less than a third live in Cornwall. The largest concentrations there are St Austell, Falmouth and Camborne-Redruth and Penzance-Newlyn where towns have grown together in spite of intense rivalry in the past. Fewer than half a dozen other places in Cornwall have more than ten thousand inhabitants. In Devon the cities of Exeter and Plymouth and the vast tourist sprawl around Torbay account for nearly half the population.

Away from the urban concentrations and the coastal resorts, therefore, the countryside is comparatively thinly populated. It is made up of extensive granite highlands and, between them and down to the coasts, steep river valleys, small towns and villages and hundreds of small and medium-sized farms. Agriculture is the main industry, though complemented now by the holiday trade. Except for certain specialised districts, this is pastoral land with large areas unsuitable for anything but grass and rough grazing. Cereals can be grown in places off the granite in Cornwall and East Cornwall has some noted dairy herds. The Tamar Valley and areas in the far South-West are well known for flowers and vegetables. In Devon the red soils of the Exe and Otter Valleys and of the South Hams produce both milk and crops. But primarily this is stock-raising country – dairy and beef cattle, sheep, pigs and hardy ponies to share the moorland grazing.

Yet the region is famous for its clotted cream, whether called Cornish or Devonshire. The reputation was made and is maintained in farmhouse and cottage kitchens, wherever a cow or two is kept, and in little village dairies rather than in the mechanised creameries. The process is simple. The milk needs to be fresh from the cow and stood in a pan for twenty-four hours in winter, twelve hours in summer. It is then heated slowly, without allowing it to boil, until it is sufficiently scalded. After a long cooling a yellowy crust forms on top, the mark of success.

Agricultural colleges at Seale-Hayne and Bicton and a Horticultural Experimental Station at Camborne feed new blood and new ideas into the farming industry. Significantly the first Young Farmers' Club in England was formed in Devon sixty years ago. Each year the importance of the industry focuses in the two great County Shows, both with permanent showgrounds: the Royal Cornwall at Wadebridge, the Devon at Exeter.

Everywhere the countryside is permeated by the sea. From Brown Willy, the highest point on Bodmin Moor, both the Atlantic and the English Channel are visible on a clear day. An explorer on the wild heights of southern Dartmoor is constantly aware of long stretches of the English Channel. No one in Devon lives more than twenty-five miles from the sea and in Cornwall more than eighteen.

Yet it was not the sea, rather the wilderness of Dartmoor, its solitude and wide horizons and long, long history, which drew me to live and work in Devon nearly forty years ago. In time the rest of the granite spine of the South-West beckoned: Bodmin Moor wreathed in mist and legend, Hensbarrow Moors where every vestige of the past has been obliterated by a compelling industrial ugliness, and then the rather undistinguished shelf known as Carnmenellis, the final stepping stone before the Land's End peninsula. All the time the land is getting lower and the sea drawing nearer

from north and south. At last, beyond Penzance and St Ives and out to the Scillies, the granite and the sea coalesce – a sort of fulfilment.

Many groups of prehistoric settlers came coastwise to the region. It is rich in their remains, particularly on those granite lumps other than Hensbarrow. Megalithic and later burials, stone circles and stone rows and standing stones abound, together with settlements and promontory forts. Prehistoric trade was seaborne, north to Wales and Ireland, south to the Continent. The boats hugged the coast until narrower seas and favourable weather enabled a safe crossing to be made. The sea routes were more important than any communication with the north-east by land. The tracks in the peninsula ran north and south from harbour to harbour, by-passing the dangerous channel round Land's End.

When the Romans advanced into the South-West a loose confederation of Celtic tribes called the Dumnonii were in occupation. The Second Augustan Legion, which had been given the task of subduing them, was probably supported by a fleet moving along the south coast. However, the archaeological evidence suggests that the Legion encountered little resistance. The Dumnonii continued to live in many of their forts, villages and farms.

The imprint of Rome is strongest east of the River Exe. A legionary fortress served as a nucleus for the only Roman city in the region, *Isca Dumnoniorum*, later to be known as Exeter. This was the administrative centre for the whole of the Dumnonii. The stone wall eventually built to defend it can be traced along most of its course, immaculate Roman masonry visible in places below the crude Saxon and later rebuilding. In East Devon sites of villas are known near Uplyme and Seaton and the great road to Bath, Cirencester and Lincoln, the Fosse Way, started from a harbour on the Axe estuary. Another road coming from

Dorchester crossed the Fosse near Axminster and went on to Honiton and Exeter.

Elsewhere the signs of Roman authority are minimal and the land west of the Exe must have been lightly held. A military road ran north of Dartmoor with forts guarding crossings of the Taw, Okement, Tamar and Camel Rivers. In Cornwall a few milestones found near the coasts probably stood on short stretches of road leading to ports where tin and other metals were exported in late Roman times. On the Exmoor coast are the remains of two first-century fortlets, apparently built to keep watch for raiders setting out from the coast of Wales, then unconquered.

Christianity became the official religion before the Romans abandoned Britain to its own devices but there is no evidence that the Dumnonii of the South-West were other than thorough pagans up to this time. It was in the centuries after the Roman withdrawal that missionaries from Wales, Ireland and Brittany came by sea to convert them and to establish the Celtic Church, never to be forgotten, especially by the Cornish.

These missionaries, the Celtic Saints, seem to have arrived by the boatload. More than two hundred church dedications in Devon and Cornwall can be traced to them, notwithstanding the ultimate triumph of the Church of Rome. Buryan, Erth, Just, Keverne, Mawgan, Tudy, Veep – a long litany of Saints' names on Cornish sign-posts warns the traveller to expect inscribed stones, holy wells and wheel-headed crosses that once marked tracks and sacred sites. The Celtic Church was monastic, with no hierarchy above the Abbot, and small communities were established on or near the coasts and estuaries in both Devon and Cornwall. Ruins on the cliff-top at Tintagel are thought to be the remains of one such community. Exposed on shelves of rock two hundred feet above the pounding of the Atlantic rollers, life must have been rigorous for these early monks.

The Saxon settlement marked the creation of Devon and Cornwall as shires. It came late, whatever raiding preceded it – Devon was not wholly occupied until AD 710 and Cornwall more than a hundred years later. By these dates the Saxons too had become Christians. The Dumnonii were defeated in battle but spared the worst ravages of the earlier heathens. And a diminishing population since Roman times meant that the peninsula offered plenty of vacant land for the Saxons to colonise without necessarily dispossessing the natives.

The eastern boundary of Devon, apart from some parish-swappings in the last century, was created by the Saxons. It follows an illogical course from an arbitrary division of Exmoor, far the greater part of which is in Somerset, to an unremarkable point on the south coast near the Dorset town of Lyme Regis. The boundary between Devon and Cornwall was fixed on the Tamar, with a mere six-mile land border between its source and the north coast at Marsland Mouth.

The Saxons made the first real effort to integrate the peninsula into England. But Celtic race and custom and language lingered on in Cornwall. The Cornish became different, regarding the Bretons and Welsh as brothers and the English as foreigners. Devon too may have had reason to regard itself as different. According to the distinguished Devon historian, Dr W. G. Hoskins, many people with pre-Saxon blood are to be found among its natives, notably along the south coast and on the edge of Dartmoor. But while Devon was brought sooner and more closely into the English structure, Cornwall's difference persisted into modern times. A thousand years of tribal life is cherished still in Cornish hearts. The Celtic Saints were never canonised by the Roman Church but the celebration of their feast days went on throughout the Middle Ages and even survived the Reformation and the Puritans. Use of the Cornish

Fishing boats reflected in the harbour at Porthleven, Mount's Bay, Cornwall.

language continued into the 18th century. The Assize Judges did not get further west than Launceston, two miles across the Tamar, before 1715 and then only in summer until Victoria's reign. For many centuries the rest of England regarded the Tamar as the limit of civilisation. The Cornish always claimed the river as their own, a symbol of independence, a defence against the English – and against the Devil who resided with them! The Devonian recognised the frontier. If he had to cross it, he threw a coin in the river to placate the 'piskies' and guarantee his safe return.

Throughout the Middle Ages and down to the 17th century the colonisation and enclosure of land, the making of new farms out of woodland and the poor soils of moor and waste, went on. The landscape gradually assumed a pattern that largely remains: small fields, often irregular in shape, climbing the hills and nudging the high moors and cliffs; hundreds of lonely farms and villages; a maze of lanes unrivalled in England. Viewed from the air many holdings still look like toy farms.

At the same time fishing and ship-building were of growing importance, also the exporting of tin and other metals and of cloth. Up to the Industrial Revolution the region was as industrialised as any other part of England. Devon had taken the lead in the revival of tin-working, which seems to have been neglected in post-Roman times, and produced nearly the whole supply for Europe in the late 12th century. Then Cornwall refound its hidden wealth and was soon exporting ten times as much as Devon. The cloth industry, however, brought great prosperity to Devon from the 14th century onwards. The splendid roof of Exeter's Guildhall and the rich embellishments of churches in wool towns like Cullompton and Tiverton still bear witness to this prosperity.

The skills of the South-West's seamen were meanwhile refined by centuries of trading, war, privateering and unashamed piracy. In the

The North Devon coastal path in the Exmoor National Park from near Hunters' Inn. The path climbs back to the cliffs along the side of Heddon's Mouth Cleave, a spectacular gorge of woods and scree gouged out by the river Heddon tumbling down from the moor to the sea.

explorations and struggles of the Tudor Age they achieved a national supremacy. A long line of sailors, from pressed men to admirals, followed. The sea is always there, and it is the sea which has drawn an ever-increasing tide of visitors for the last two hundred years.

The generally mild climate, when the time was ripe, also attracted visitors. Penzance owes its repute as a resort to the same conditions that produce the earliest flowers and vegetables grown on the mainland of England; only those from the Scillies are earlier. But rainfall is heavy overall and gales often sweep the exposed peninsula. 'Devon, O Devon in wind and rain' rings true. Favoured resorts on the south coast have only thirty inches of rain a year but inland the fall increases dramatically. Dartmoor averages over eighty inches. The disaster that overwhelmed the small north coast resort of Lynmouth at the height of the holiday season in 1952 was caused by nine inches of rain falling on Exmoor in one day. The river Lyn swept away bridges and destroyed or damaged a hundred buildings; thirty people died. Blizzards in the winters of 1946-7 and 1962-3 killed hundreds of head of stock and brought great hardship to most of the region. Twice in the last five years exceptional conditions have isolated villages and many farms for long periods. But normally spells of extreme weather are brief.

Gales and turbulent seas have left a long history of shipwrecks along the coasts. The old jingle
> From Padstow Point to Lundy Light,
> A watery grave by day and night

sums up the dangers of the Atlantic coast, but the south coast also has claimed many victims. Today a comprehensive rescue organisation exists: coastguards, police, lifeboats, the RN and RAF Search and Rescue teams. Henry Trengrouse of Helston invented the rocket apparatus which revolutionised life-saving at sea early in the last century. Now the helicopter, with its winch and devoted crews, supplements the heroism of lifeboatmen.

The historic occupations of fishing, mining and the woollen industry declined in importance. Most of the mills closed one after another during the 19th century, though notably the carpet factory at Axminster has revived. The pilchard and herring shoals, which once yielded enormous catches, have vanished. Brixham in Devon and Newlyn in Cornwall are commercial fishing ports, but generally the industry is on a smaller scale than in the past. For every registered fishing vessel there are a hundred pleasure boats.

By the middle of the last century mining, especially for tin and copper, had reached its peak and hundreds of mines were in operation. Only three are worked today. Derelict buildings, spoil heaps and abandoned shafts are a landscape feature, particularly in West Cornwall, the Tamar valley and on Dartmoor. The Cornish names are redolent of other days: Botallack, Levant, Dolcoath, Tresavean and many others. Mining harnessed the native inventive genius. Humphry Davy, whose safety lamp saved many lives in coal mines elsewhere, came from Penzance. A Devonian, Thomas Newcomen, invented the steam pumping engine but it was the great Richard Trevithick of Illogan who, among his many achievements, perfected it. The Cornish beam engine enabled the mines to be pushed deeper than ever before. Yet another Cornishman, William Bickford, designed the safety fuse for blasting. Devon also has its share of abandoned workings like the vast complex of Devon Great Consols in the Tamar valley and on Dartmoor Wheal Emma, Vitifer and many others. Tin and copper in huge quantities, also lead, manganese, silver-lead, iron, wolfram and arsenic, were wrung from the lodes until cheaper supplies became available overseas. The ruins are monuments to a working life as short, hard and dangerous as any, and to the thousands of miners who emigrated all over the world when the mines closed. The Camborne School of Mines with its international reputation is a continuing by-product of the once great industry.

Quarries, abandoned and active, also mark the landscape and have a long history. Stone was dug by the Romans in the quarries at Beer, which continued to be used at intervals down to Victorian times. Delabole, allegedly the largest slate quarry in England, was first exploited under the Tudors and has become a tourist attraction. Granite, limestone (much for agricultural use), sand, gravel, roadstone and railway ballast are all extracted but the most significant quarrying today is for china clay and, in the Bovey Basin, ball or potters' clay. China clay was discovered in Cornwall about 1756 by a Devon Quaker, William Cookworthy, perhaps better known as the first maker of hard paste porcelain in England. The industry developed slowly at first but is now of national importance. Grey mud or dust smearing roads and hedgerows and discolouring streams and rivers, the towering grey-white heaps of quartz waste must be endured for the sake of these valuable exports.

Boat-building continues at many small yards. Recent products have been a replica of the *Mayflower* which re-enacted the crossing of the Atlantic in 1620 and the trimaran sailed by Chay Blyth and Ron James to victory in the Transatlantic Race of 1981. Every coastal and estuary port has yards to maintain commercial boats and the vast new fleets of yachts, cabin cruisers and sailing boats. At Falmouth major repairs to ships are carried out. The Naval Dockyard at Devonport, with nearly three hundred years of history, continues to be of vital importance. It is appropriate that the world-famous Marine Research Laboratory should be situated close to Plymouth Sound and that a fine Maritime Museum has given new meaning to Exeter's deserted quays and warehouses.

Other industrial activities, including paper-mills, potteries and many kinds of small engineering, are numerous but on a small scale compared with china clay. Visitors with the idea that all is 'cream and cider' would be surprised at the enterprises to be found on the new industrial estates of the larger towns and tucked away in many of the smaller ones. Some firms moved to the region during the Second World War and have remained; some are more recent arrivals which places as large as Plymouth and as small as Bodmin have set out to attract.

A few typical industries have not yet been squeezed out. Down on the Lizard ornaments and souvenirs have been made from the beautiful serpentine rock for more than a hundred years and remain popular. Honiton still makes a little lace, a reminder of a once flourishing cottage industry all over East Devon. Cider-making in Devon, with records going back to the 13th century, has also sadly declined. Centralised production, as in the case of beer, has finished off all but two or three of the many small factories that once existed. The potent 'scrumpy' is still made on many farms, both for farm use and for sale, but some orchards are old and are not being renewed.

In contrast, the making of the famous Cornish pasty flourishes though some products scarcely deserve the name. The genuine pasty consists of chunks of raw beef and potato, with or without onion and sometimes with turnip. They are baked in a circle of pastry folded over them and crimped at the curving edge. The meat should not be minced nor the pasty eaten with a knife and fork. Held in the hand it should be devoured vertically from one end to the other. A napkin or paper bag retains the warmth and protects the fingers. Properly made and fresh from the oven, the Cornish pasty is a treat.

Tourism, the other major industry of the South-West, began a mere two hundred years ago,

Crantock Beach, half a mile wide and backed by
dunes, is typical of many sandy coves along the
North Cornish coast. Below the right-hand cliff the
Gannel river slips almost unnoticed into the sea.

developing in partnership with roads and railways and then again with roads. Up to about 1750 few wheeled vehicles were in use in Devon, let alone Cornwall. Travel by water was still easier and quicker than by land. People rode horseback and most goods were carried by pack-horses, heavy goods on sleds drawn by horses or oxen. No one travelled far for pleasure. Then the turnpike trusts were founded to improve the roads. The first in Devon brought the London road to Exeter. Others soon followed.

The development of the seaside resorts was also encouraged by medical opinion, which advocated the benefits of sea air and bathing, and by the wars with France between 1793 and 1815 which prevented the upper classes from travelling on the Continent. Well-to-do citizens of Exeter were already taking the short trip to the fine beach at Exmouth for diversion and bathing. By 1800 Exmouth's attractions were known elsewhere and it may well claim to be the first resort in Devon.

Sidmouth, Dawlish and Teignmouth were not far behind. The use of Torbay by the fleet during the Wars (Plymouth Sound could be a dangerous harbour at times until Rennie's massive breakwater was completed in 1840) turned the hamlet of Tor Quay into a town. Its population trebled in twenty years, long before the coming of the railway. On the north coast the first hotel at Lynmouth opened in 1807; Ilfracombe began to change from a small market town and port after the French Wars, visitors arriving by boat from Bristol. But generally the holiday business in Devon developed hand in hand with the vast improvement in vehicles and road conditions.

The Cornish resorts had to wait for the arrival of the railway. The line from Bristol reached Exeter in 1844 and fifteen years later Brunel's great bridge over the Tamar at Saltash firmly linked Cornwall to the rest of England. During the next forty years Penzance, Falmouth, Newquay and

St Ives became established as resorts. The railway and the gradual spread of holidays brought drastic changes. Newquay, once a fishing village of a hundred people, has grown steadily into a town of nearly fifteen thousand residents living by tourism. With the decline of mining the visitors were a boon to Cornwall, however much it continued to cherish its proud independence.

The impact of the motor car was already felt before the Second World War. A bypass to take traffic away from the heart of Exeter was opened in the Thirties and became notorious for its jams in the summer. But the complete take-over by road traffic has occurred since the War, compounded by the decay of the once comprehensive railway system. The *coup de grâce* has been the opening of the motorway which thrusts like a spear into the heart of Devon. It is difficult to assess the real effect of this but millions more people are within a few hours' driving time of the region's resorts. Visitors can pour in by road faster than ever before.

And why should they not come? The region offers a wonderful environment and nearly every form of outdoor recreation, including such rarities in England as surfing and shark-fishing.

It is estimated that over six million people a year come to relax and enjoy themselves in Devon and Cornwall. Mini-peaks at Easter and the Spring Bank Holiday are followed by massive invasions from June to September. The two counties probably share the influx about equally. Cornwall therefore sustains more visitors to each resident and square mile, but Devon, in addition to its own visitors, bears the brunt of the traffic passing through to Cornwall. Recent surveys suggest that a small majority of the resident population consider the advantages of tourism outweigh its drawbacks – the money that visitors spend condones all. But attitudes vary greatly. The inhabitants of the resorts who live by tourism have little in common with country-dwellers who endure many of the nuisances with little or no reciprocal advantage. Overall it must be accepted that the tourist industry is vital to the economy of the region.

Apart from the inevitable traffic congestion during the season, the industry creates a problem for the Water Authority. With the population at resorts doubling and trebling, and consuming an amazing one hundred million gallons of water a day, sites for new reservoirs are continually being sought. Wherever the Authority looks a bitter controversy rages. If it chooses the high moors, where several reservoirs exist already, the champions of the environment resist. It is only necessary to look at the Avon Dam on Dartmoor, which has ruined a beautiful valley and reduced the river to a sorry stream, to see the environmental damage caused by high-level reservoirs. If the Authority chooses land off the moors, the agricultural industry hastens to the barricades. It is equally unacceptable that farm land should be lost simply to satisfy the exceptional demands of the holiday months. The great majority of visitors throng to the coasts, so a determined effort should surely be made to overcome the problems of using sea-water.

The loss of agricultural land, the penetration of heavier and heavier lorries into the countryside, the threat of oil pollution to the coast – all these national problems seem particularly disastrous in this most rural of areas with its rich and varied scenery and wild life and its wonderful coastline. The future of the region can be summed up simply: how is this coastal and rural wealth to be preserved against the pressures of industry? Is the creation of Nature Reserves, both national and local, the designation of 'Heritage Coasts' and 'Areas of Outstanding Natural Beauty', of National and Countryside Parks, enough? The National Trust and many vigorous local organisations contribute actively to the defence of the environment, so do some enlightened people in local government. Are the scales weighted against them? As the history of the South-West shows, industries go up and down but rarely stand still. The demands of successful industries will go on and on. Is it possible that one day the visitors will cease to come because the region has allowed its coast and countryside to be destroyed?

A strong and forward-looking agricultural industry, working not against the conservationists but in harmony with them, is the best hope for the future. Both must play their part as guardians of this precious environment. If the South-West is to continue to serve the rest of the country as a holiday paradise then grandiose ideas for new roads, new industries and the relocation of old ones must be strictly controlled.

The visitors, who have become so essential to the region, obviously do damage to the environment. This is unavoidable wherever thousands of cars and people congregate. The peak year was 1978;

numbers have decreased slightly each year since. This check may not be a bad thing. It would be a disaster if the numbers of visitors escalated beyond the capacity of the region to contain them.

The holiday industry has one advantage over others: it is mainly seasonal. When the campers and caravaners and the rest depart, autumn brings a measure of relief to the South-West. The barns are stacked; pasture and stubble and the empty beaches, the moors and steep-sided valleys and headlands smoulder with a weary contentment. Months lie ahead in which the peninsula can recover its poise and renew itself, ready to offer next year its natural attractions and its welcome. So long as this happens there is hope.

Agriculture goes on every day of the year. So must the struggle to preserve the region's wild life and environment. For these are important not only to the people living here but to the well-being of people living in every part of our country.

Paul Pettit

Marwood House, Honiton (*opposite, top*), was built in 1619 for John Marwood, a son of Queen Elizabeth's physician.

Boats on the shingle at Beer (*opposite, bottom*) recall centuries of fishing and smuggling before the tourists came.

The beautifully maintained interior of St Andrew's church, Cullompton (*below*), has a painted wagon roof, contrasting with the grey Beer stone of the nave arcades, and a fine rood-screen.

A horse-drawn barge (*below*) takes passengers along the Grand Western Canal. In 1971 the Devon County Council, vigorously prodded by a local committee of conservationists, took over the eleven-mile stretch from Tiverton to the Devon/Somerset border and made it the county's first Countryside Park.

Old Blundell's School, Tiverton (*opposite, top*), built in 1604, was converted to dwellings about 1880 when the school moved to its present location less than a mile away. Peter Blundell, the founder, was a wealthy clothier of the town. John Ridd is found at school here in the opening chapters of *Lorna Doone*. The building was eventually purchased by the Old Boys Association and is now in the hands of the National Trust.

The Dart Valley Railway from Buckfastleigh to Totnes (*opposite, bottom*) is run privately as a summer attraction for steam enthusiasts and visitors. Lovingly restored trains puff joyously up and down one of the loveliest valleys in Devon.

The library at Killerton, Broad Clyst (*left*), the Georgian mansion of one of Devon's best known families, the Aclands. It was said at one time that they could ride from North to South Devon on their own land. The Privy Council uniforms, one belonging to the Aclands and one from the Paulise de Bush costume collection housed at Killerton, were part of a recent exhibition put on by the National Trust.

Gleaming white between its red cliffs, Sidmouth (*below*) has an air of modest dignity seldom found in seaside resorts. Even its river is modest, a mere six miles in length and reaching the sea unobtrusively under the far cliff. Early visitors were Jane Austen (1801) and in the winter of 1819-20 the Duke and Duchess of Kent with their infant daughter, Victoria. Between these dates the population doubled and the early 19th-century domestic buildings give Sidmouth its style. For one fortnight each year the town erupts uncharacteristically with an International Folk Dance Festival.

A stream runs beside the main street of Otterton village (*opposite*) where typical cob-and-thatch cottages adjoin others of stone and slate.

Thatched buildings reflected in a placid River Exe at Bickleigh Bridge between Exeter and Tiverton. A bridge has existed here since Tudor times, the present one a rebuilding in the last century after damage by floods. The popular Trout Inn occupies the long building on the left.

Hayes Barton (*below*), birthplace of Sir Walter Raleigh, is an E-shaped Tudor house in a green valley near East Budleigh.

Silos for imported grain at Exmouth (*opposite*, *top*). The harbour can only take ships up to 1,000 tons and tourism, rather than shipping, dominates the oldest of Devon's resorts.

The port of Topsham (*opposite*, *bottom*) on the Exe. Sailing has taken over the waterfront yet not quite ousted salmon fishing carried on here since the 12th century. Topsham mustered ships against the Armada and is so full of historic buildings that the whole town is a Conservation Area.

Except for its distinctive Norman towers, Exeter Cathedral is the supreme example of Decorated style, built in a mere ninety years from 1275. The porches, images and great window of the west front (*below*) were the final flourish. The great vault (*opposite*), unique in England, stretches unbroken over nave and chancel to give the Cathedral a spaciousness beyond its mere dimensions. The vault bosses are masterpieces of 14th-century stone carving.

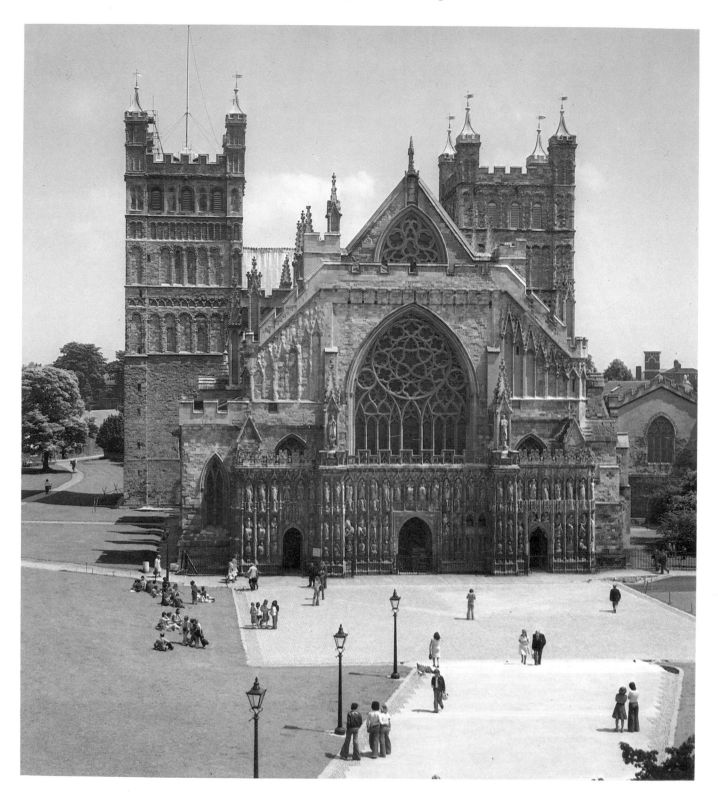

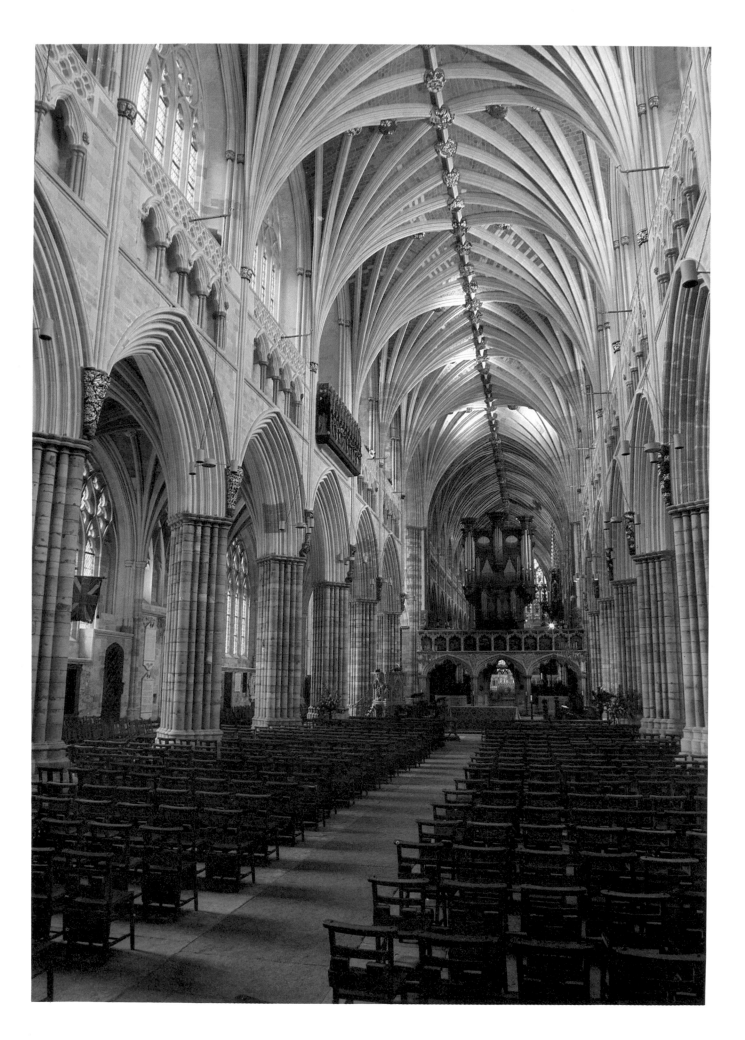

The early-14th-century gatehouse and south wall
of Berry Pomeroy castle. In 1548 the Pomeroys
sold it to Edward Seymour, Duke of Somerset. The
Seymours added the great Tudor mansion which
rises behind the earlier curtain wall. Abandoned in
the 17th century, the castle is a romantic ruin on a
narrow spur surrounded by woods – still the
property of the Seymours, only the second family
to own it since the Norman Conquest.

Dawlish, one of the early 'watering places', takes its name from the 'black stream' that flows through it. The old village was nearly a mile inland but, as it grew in the first decade of the 19th century, the stream and ground down to the shore were landscaped to form pleasant lawns and artificial waterfalls. In sheltered valleys near the town the famous Devon violets are grown.

The building with its water wheel by the river at Bovey Tracey was never a mill. Built about 1850 as stables with servants' quarters above, the wheel raised water from the river Bovey to a slate cistern for use by the stables and nearby Riverside House. In many small places in Devon formerly disused buildings can be found restored and adapted for light industry, in this instance for the manufacture of electronic components.

The front at Teignmouth, looking south-west towards the river mouth and across to the prominent red cliff known as the Ness. Another of Devon's older resorts, Keats stayed here for a few weeks in 1818 and complained half-humourously of the Devon weather. It is also a port from which the valuable ball or potters' clay of the Teign valley is exported to many European countries.

The tramway near Haytor, Dartmoor (*left*), was made of granite blocks three to eight feet long, laid end to end and flanged to form rails. The line opened in 1820 to carry granite from the quarries on Haytor Down to a canal in the Teign valley, a well-engineered descent of 1,300 feet in seven miles. Much of the granite was shipped from Teignmouth for use on public buildings in London.

Grimspound (*below*), one of many Bronze Age settlements on Dartmoor. The substantial wall encloses four acres and contains the foundations of twenty-four buildings and traces of stock pens. Unfortunately a public bridle-way has been allowed to pass through the settlement and the consequent erosion is clearly visible.

Bowerman's Nose, Hayne Down (*opposite*), said to resemble a human form. The 'natural monuments' of Dartmoor National Park, nearly 200 of them, are believed to have been formed by weathering and erosion of the surrounding granite leaving the tors and rock piles exposed and clatters of dislodged rocks spread on the slopes below.

The bold outline of Hound Tor, with Hay Tor beyond, seen from Hayne Down.

Castle Drogo, Drewsteignton (*below*), was built by
Sir Edwin Lutyens between 1911 and 1930 for
Julius Drewe, who had retired from business at the
age of 33 after founding the Home & Colonial
Stores. Local granite was used throughout. The site
on a promontory above the wooded gorge of the
river Teign is worthy of any genuine castle. A
country house on this scale is unlikely ever to be
attempted again and the National Trust acquired
Castle Drogo and opened it to the public in 1975.

A herd of ponies on Dartmoor (*opposite*). The
introduction of alien stallions and the resulting
cross-breeding means that only a few pure-bred
Dartmoor ponies run on the Moor – stallions for a
'rest' or mares already safely in foal. But something
of the strain remains in many of the mixed herds
roaming the waste. After the autumn 'drifts' or
round-ups, sales (but not of pure-bred ponies)
take place at border markets.

Crockern Tor Farm, Two Bridges, Dartmoor
(*opposite, top*), is a bleak place when snow lies for
weeks on end.

Wistman's wood (*opposite, bottom*), one of
Dartmoor's ancient copses, has a weird, even
sinister, appearance. Twisted, stunted oaks struggle
among rocks to survive the acid soil, a heavy
rainfall and browsing animals.

Okehampton Castle (*below*) controlled the routes
north of Dartmoor and was the only castle in
Devon recorded in the Domesday survey.

Stone and thatch in a sheltered combe, Buckland-
in-the-Moor near Ashburton. From the village the
ground plunges down to the river Webburn and
the horseshoe gorge of the Dart; and up steeply to
one of Dartmoor's best known landmarks,
Buckland Beacon (1,280 ft), with awesome
views and the Ten Commandments carved
on a granite block.

William Crossing's great *Guide to Dartmoor* (1909)
records some thirty clapper bridges on the moor.
The oldest go back to the 13th century when
medieval farmers and tin-workers made bridges for
themselves and their pack-animals. Lonely
Huntingdon clapper, shown below, probably dates
from the 17th century, when a house and
newtake, or enclosure, were in existence nearby,
or from the early 19th century when Huntingdon
Warren was enclosed.

The river Dart at Totnes (*below*). From the quay
below the bridge steamers leave in summer for
Dartmouth, passing some of the choicest river
scenery in England. The town is a story in stone:
Norman castle and town walls, the latter on
Saxon foundations; butterwalks and a famous
gate across the steep main street; a 15th-century
church and even older Guildhall – and it is
a pleasant place to live.

A prosperous Cistercian Abbey in the Dart valley
for 400 years, Buckfast (*opposite*) was despoiled at
the Dissolution. The Benedictines acquired the site
in the 19th century and the erection of a new
church by the monks themselves began in 1907. It
was finally consecrated in 1932, a building in
Norman and Early English style on the site of the
medieval Abbey church.

A herd of Devon cattle passes through Cockington
(*opposite, top*), a well-preserved thatched village
only a mile inland from Torbay.

Sheep judging at the Totnes Show (*opposite, bottom*).
Wool brought wealth to Devon for centuries up to
the Industrial Revolution, and sheep are still
important in the economy for wool and meat.

Night scene at Torquay (*above*) – the illuminated
Pavilion beside the harbour.

Fishing boats in Brixham harbour (*opposite*).
Historically it was the most important fishing port
in Devon and is so today. William of Orange
landed here in 1688 and his statue on the Quay
records his intentions – 'the liberties of England and
the Protestant religion I will maintain.' The Rev.
H. F. Lyte, author of 'Abide with me', lived on the
slopes of Berry Head, which protects the harbour
from the east.

Oldway, Paignton (*above*), a mansion of more than
a hundred rooms, now used for local authority
offices and functions. In *The Buildings of England*
Pevsner compares it to an American millionaire's
house and it was indeed built (1874-1904) for the
Singer sewing-machine family. In the extensive
gardens minature box hedges contrast with the
massive Ionic columns of the east facade.

Prawle Point (*right*), the southernmost tip of the South Hams and of Devon, seen in the distance from Start Point. Many species of butterfly flourish in the mild climate of this stretch of the coast and over 200 species of birds have been recorded in recent years. At sea the sighting of grey seals, basking sharks and porpoises can be a bonus for the bird-watcher.

The entrance to the anchorage at the mouth of the river Dart was guarded by castles at Kingswear on the east bank and Dartmouth on the west. A chain could be slung between them when danger threatened. Dartmouth Castle (*below*) is mainly 15th century and strangely dwarfed by St Petrock's Church beside it. The castle has gun-ports and slits for muskets as well as the large, timber-framed opening through which the chain passed. From Dartmouth came Chaucer's Shipmaster, thought to be a portrait of John Hawley, the greatest of the port's medieval tycoons.

Another view of the South Ham's coast, looking
northwards over Torcross and along the sand-and-
shingle ridge between Slapton Ley, a large
freshwater Nature Reserve on the left, and Slapton
Sands and the waters of Start Bay right. A small
monument on the ridge commemorates the use of
the area for battle practice by the United States
Army before the invasion of Normandy. All
traces of the havoc then wrought have
happily disappeared.

Saltram House overlooks the Plym estuary and was acquired with its contents by the National Trust in 1957. Contemporary architecture and furnishings are combined in Robert Adam's grand saloon (*opposite*), a double cube and a near-perfect example of 18th-century design. The Axminster carpet was specially woven to reflect the ceiling. Four portraits on the walls are by Reynolds who often stayed with the Parker family at Saltram.

Tavistock (*above*), one of the medieval Stannary towns where tin was weighed and stamped before sale, expanded and was largely rebuilt in the 19th century as a result of the copper boom. It has always been the centre for a large agricultural district. The picture shows the 15th-century parish church, dedicated unusually to St Eustace, and behind it one of the many splendid viaducts that had to be built when the railway engineers encountered the steep valleys of the region.

The two bridges across the Tamar at Saltash which
have rivetted Cornwall to the rest of England. The
railway bridge was one of Brunel's many
masterpieces. He died soon after it was opened by
Prince Albert in 1859. The suspension bridge for
road traffic, completed 102 years later, produced a
two-way revolution: Cornish people could reach
the shops and entertainments of Plymouth and
visitors could stream into Cornwall without
the inevitable and memorable delays of the old
Saltash car ferry.

(*Left*) A portrait of Drake, his Drum and a model of the Golden Hind displayed at Buckland Abbey near Yelverton. The Abbey church was converted into a mansion by Sir Richard Grenville of *Revenge* fame and sold in 1581 to Drake who lived there when not at sea. It is National Trust property managed by Plymouth Corporation as a Drake, Naval and Folk Museum.

Plymouth Hoe (*below*) from the Citadel ramparts, on one side the Sound and on the other the City, far and away the largest in the region. The Hoe must be reckoned among the outstanding scenic and historic places of England. To question that Drake finished his game of bowls hereabouts before tackling the Armada is treason. On the Hoe are Smeaton's Lighthouse, re-erected after 120 years service on the Eddystone Rocks, the tall Naval War Memorial and of course a statue of Drake. The base for so many voyages of exploration, Plymouth has given its name to cities all over the world.

The church of St Michael, Brentor, on its hunk of
volcanic rock, a famous landmark in West Devon.
All over Christendom chapels and churches
dedicated to the Archangel were built on the tops of
hills (*see* pages 66 and 78–9 for other examples).
Risdon in his *Survey of Devon* (1630) was blunt:
'a church full bleak and weather beaten, all alone, as
it were forsaken, whose churchyard doth hardly
afford depth of earth to bury the dead . . .'

On the main road to North and West Cornwall the
first place across the Tamar is the hilltop town of
Launceston, the so-called 'Gateway to Cornwall'.
The exterior of the church of St Mary Magdalene,
built in 1511 to 1524, is profusely decorated. At the
east end a recumbent Magdalene was hacked from
the obstinate granite. The rather rough execution
was due to the material, not to lack of piety.

The Great Hall at Cotehele (*below*), built on the Cornish side of the Tamar valley about 1515. The estate belonged to the Edgcumbe family and was the first historic house to pass to the National Trust after being accepted by the Treasury in satisfaction of estate duty. With its original furniture, armour and tapestries it is the most impressive Tudor house in Cornwall.

Wild flowers on Rame Head (*opposite*) south-west of Plymouth.

Siblyback Reservoir on Bodmin Moor was opened in 1969 and serves the area of Liskeard and south-east Cornwall. Its 140 surface acres are extensively used for recreation – canoeing, sailing, board-sailing and strictly controlled water-skiing in addition to fishing. Provision is also made for bird-watching. All this is some compensation for the loss of one more moorland valley.

Looking north-west from Rame Head the three-mile sandy stretch of Whitsand Bay is deceptively beautiful. Strong currents and fast-moving tides proved disastrous for many fine ships trying to enter Plymouth in the days of sail. From Rame Head the Eddystone Lighthouse can sometimes be seen, ten miles out to sea. Except for periodic maintenance the lighthouse, which replaced Smeaton's (page 55) in 1882, is worked from the mainland.

The entrance to the harbour at Polperro on the south Cornish coast.

A cottage at Polperro decorated with shells and having the typical outside staircase of many of the buildings which climb higgledy-piggledy above each other on the hillsides above the harbour. After centuries of self-sufficiency and isolation visitors swamp Polperro in summer and, as elsewhere in the region, dependence on fishing, smuggling and salvage from the sea is a thing of the past.

Fisherman mending nets at East Looe with West Looe in the background. Fishing-luggers still sail out of the harbour, but in summer pleasure trips by sea to Fowey or Polperro and fishing for sport, particularly shark-fishing, are more important.

(*Opposite*) The church tower of the ancient seaport of Fowey looking across the river to the wooded slopes of Bodinnick. It is still a busy port and one of the most attractive places in Cornwall, comparatively unscarred by tourism.

In mid-Cornwall the ruined chapel on top of
Roche Rock was dedicated, as customary (page 56),
to St Michael. The rock rises 100 feet above marsh,
grassland and stone walls on one hand and china
clay quarries on the other. For Roche is a clay
village at the edge of a large spread of workings.
Granite steps, then ladders, give access to the
chapel and a view which would surprise the
medieval hermit.

China clay workings cover vast areas round
St Austell (and elsewhere in the region). Cornwall
has always had to exploit its underground wealth to
survive. The imposing ugliness of the clay quarries
is merely another chapter in a long story. Today
the chimneys and engine-houses of abandoned tin
and copper mines are considered worthy of
preservation. Will the same attitude apply one day
to these gigantic gougings and spoil heaps?

One of the round cottages at Veryan (*below*), a pleasant village on the edge of the Roseland Peninsula (page 72). A cottage stands in the centre of the village and two at each end. Erected early in the 19th century by Hugh Rowe, a builder of Lostwithiel, they look as though they should be older, but have already acquired a legend. Having no north wall, it is said, the Devil cannot enter them or the village.

Mevagissey (*opposite*), like Polperro, is an ancient fishing village transformed into a popular resort. In the old days pilchards by the ton were caught and exported to Mediterranean countries. The Navy also took supplies of what the sailors christened 'Mevagissey Ducks'.

Trelissick Gardens (*below*) on the Fal belong to the
National Trust and are well-known for
rhododendrons, azaleas, more than a hundred kinds
of hydrangea and many other shrubs and fine trees.
The view southwards down the river is to
Carrick Roads, one of the best deep-water
anchorages in the world.

(*Opposite*) The west front of Truro Cathedral,
consecrated 1887. The two fine towers were
completed later and are known as 'Alexandra' and
'Edward VII'. Before the creation of the diocese of
Truro in 1876, Cornwall had reluctantly formed
part of Exeter diocese for more than 800 years.
Truro is therefore one of the youngest of our
Cathedral cities but it was a thriving port and
market town for centuries before the natural
advantages of Falmouth were recognised and its
maritime importance ceased.

The peninsula east of Carrick Roads and the River Fal is called Roseland, a district which has never known a railway or a trunk road and which is divided by many sheltered wooded creeks. The church of St Just (*opposite, top*) stands on the steep slope above one of the creeks, the lych-gate level with the top of the tower. Many flowering shrubs and sub-tropical plants grow in the churchyard.

St Mawes, the 'capital of Roseland' (*opposite, bottom*), is a largely unspoilt resort and yachting centre which originally developed beside its Renaissance castle. Across Carrick Roads the low profile of Pendennis Castle on its headland completed the anchorage's seaward defences.

(*Above*) The oddly rectangular tower of Falmouth church above the harbour with Trefusis Point and Carrick Roads in the background. The other aspect of Falmouth is the holiday resort which turns its back on the harbour's activities and faces south-east to the open sea.

Helford sits snugly in its own wooded creek on the
south side of the Helford River. A ferry crosses the
estuary in summer to Helford Passage, from one
pub to another as many have observed. 'Helford'
oysters are well-known. They breed in other
rivers, but many are fattened in the beds belonging
to the oyster farm at Port Navas on another creek
of the Helford.

Lizard Point, the southernmost tip of the mainland. Under the cliff lies the disused lifeboat house and slipway. Six hundred lives were saved during the lifeboat's century of existence. The two-towered lighthouse was erected in 1752, but only one light is now used. The first coal-burning light, established early in the 17th century by Sir John Killigrew, ceased operating when opposed by Trinity House and by the local people who relied on salvage to ease their poverty.

Boats at Porthleven, Mounts Bay, a small fishing
town (population 3,000) which has tried hard to
expand into a port. Ship-building and repairing,
fishing, canning, and handling cargoes have been
carried on with varying success over the last 160
years. Recently, as in so many small places, reliance
on tourism has become dominant.

Mullion Cove on the Lizard Peninsula with its 'toy' harbour wedged against the rocks. It looks so safe and peaceful, but presents a different aspect when south-westerly gales drive the sea over the harbour walls. It is owned by the National Trust and the whole of the Lizard Peninsula has been declared an Area of Outstanding Natural Beauty.

St Michael's Mount is reached by causeway at low tide, at other times by boat.

A performance at the Minack Theatre, Porthcurno.
Stage and auditorium are fashioned out of the cliff
and back-stage the rocks fall precipitously to the
sea. The theatre opened in 1932 with, appropriately,
a production of *The Tempest*. In the distance is the
headland of Treryn-Dinas (National Trust) with a
famous rocking stone which Lieut Goldsmith RN
and a party of sailors dislodged in 1824. He was
ordered to replace it at his own expense.

Chysauster Iron Age village between Penzance and
St Ives was occupied during the first three
centuries AD, before and during Roman times. It
consists of eight houses with courtyards and nearby
a ruined *fogou* and a field system. *Fogous*, in England
peculiar to West Cornwall, are basically trenches
lined with stone walling and covered with stone
slabs and the excavated soil. They were probably
food stores like our later cellars and ice-houses.

(*Left*) The graceful sweep of Whitesand Bay in the Land's End peninsula looking south to the jetty and lifeboat station at Sennen Cove below the headland of Pedn-men-du. Beyond, the Longships lighthouse rises out of the sea a mile west of Land's End, that emotive spot which is totally commercialised and not as compelling visually as a score of other promontories in the region.

(*Above*) The Celtic Cross on Penhale Sands near Perranporth is a simple one, its decoration four holes in the circular head. It was mentioned in a charter of AD 930. Most of Cornwall's surviving crosses were erected in Saxon times and were richly carved. They marked burial places and trackways and can also be interpreted as silent protests against Saxon domination.

The entrance to the chambered tomb at Bant's
Carn, St Mary's, Isles of Scilly, a fine example of
the fifty or so megalithic tombs which have
survived on the islands. It is remarkable not only
that the Scillies contain about one fifth of all such
tombs in England and Wales but that with other
types of burial, settlements, field boundaries,
standing stones and promontory forts they are
richer in prehistoric remains than any other
comparable area.

Abbey Gardens, Tresco, cluster round the 19th–
century Abbey House built on the site of the
medieval Abbey. Begun with a nucleus of plants
from Kew, they have since expanded with
specimens acquired from all over the tropics and
the southern hemisphere. Nothing could provide a
greater contrast to the mainland's formal gardens.
Thousands of trees, shrubs and plants jostle with
tropical abandon behind the shelter belts grown to
protect them from the Atlantic gales.

Cape Cornwall (*left*) near St Just-in-Penwith is the only headland in England called a 'cape'. The chimney on the summit was part of a mine closed a hundred years ago. Many ships have foundered on the rocks offshore, the Brisons.

Lanyon Quoit (*above*) between Morvah and Madron, the remains of a chambered tomb restored in 1824 using the equipment that had replaced the rocking stone at Treryn-Dinas (page 80). Originally the stones stood at one end of a barrow thirty yards long and were higher so that a horseman could ride upright under the enormous capstone. It is one of many neolithic tombs (3rd millenium BC) in West Cornwall with similarities to those in the Isles of Scilly (page 84).

The ruins of Botallack mine, north of Cape
Cornwall, evoke all the abandoned workings of the
Land's End peninsula. The engine-house stands
boldly above the Atlantic waves. Tin, copper and
arsenic were extracted for a hundred years up to the
First World War, the workings running far out
under the sea. Geevor, a mile away, is the only
mine now operating in West Cornwall.

The village of Zennor between Land's End and St Ives in its setting of small fields marked out by stone hedges and in the background the sea. The medieval church contains the famous bench end (now part of a seat in the chancel) of the mermaid who lured a young blood of the village from the church to her home on the sea bed in nearby Pendour Cove.

St Ives harbour
protected by the pier
built by Smeaton in
1767-70 and since
lengthened. The older
houses of this important
fishing and market town
climb the hill above the
harbour. Fine beaches
enabled St Ives to
change easily to a
successful resort when
the railway arrived
and the pilchards
disappeared. It has also
attracted many artists
including the sculptress
Barbara Hepworth and
Bernard Leach the
pottery-designer and
maker.

(*Opposite, top*) Godrevy lighthouse silhouetted on its island four miles north-west of St Ives.

Gwennap Pit near Redruth (*opposite, bottom*), an old mine working where John Wesley preached many times to huge congregations. A Whit Monday service has commemorated this every year since 1806.

The restored winding engine (*below*) at East Pool between Camborne and Redruth is another memorial to the mining industry.

Newquay is the largest resort on the north Cornish coast, devoted exclusively to the holiday trade and offering all the amenities from bowls and golf to surfing and shark-fishing. The cliffs and beaches are spectacular and include the island reached by a small suspension bridge. The past is represented by Bronze Age barrows on the cliffs and a ruined hut on the hill above the harbour where watch was kept for the pilchard shoals.

Trerice near Newquay. The late Tudor house has
been faithfully restored by the National Trust. The
east facade with its mullioned windows and five
alternating gables has a look of solid serenity. The
window to the left of the entrance porch contains
576 panes of glass and lights the Hall which
occupies two floors. The home of one of Cornwall's
famous families, the Arundells, it makes an
interesting comparison with the rather humble
birthplace of Raleigh (page 26).

The stern of a small boat in the churchyard at St
Mawgan, four miles from Newquay, poignantly
recalls the dangers of the sea. In westerly gales ships
cannot find a safe haven on the Atlantic coast.
During the 19th century a thousand ships
foundered between Hartland Point and Land's End.
Notwithstanding technical advances in ships and
navigation the demands for rescue have increased,
one reason being the escalating numbers of small,
privately owned craft.

Padstow lifeboat heads out to sea, her radio aerials
raised and her crew at their stations. She has earned
an unusual tribute: the composer Malcolm Arnold
has called one of his marches 'Padstow Lifeboat'.
The service has had to adapt to changing conditions
by providing faster offshore boats and a new
inshore fleet of inflatables to cope with the
increasing numbers of holiday-makers – cliff-
climbers as well as people in boats – who get
into trouble.

Bedruthan Steps, a series of detached rocks on the coast between Newquay and Padstow seen fully exposed at low tide. The National Trust has repaired and maintains the steps cut in the cliff which give access to the beach. One of the rocks is nicknamed 'Queen Bess', another 'Samaritan' after a ship full of cotton and silks which foundered here in 1846. Local people whose clothes' closets benefited from the wreck called her the 'Good Samaritan'.

(*Below*) Flower-decked musicians and singers accompany the 'Hobby Hoss' as he prances and ambles through the streets of Padstow on May Day – a lusty, intensely local celebration of fertile summer's arrival without thought of financial gain or concession to 'foreigners'.

Unite, all unite! Let us all unite!
For summer is acome to-day –
And whither we are going, let us all unite
On the merry morning of May.

(*Opposite, top*) Surfing at Trevone Bay near Padstow. This exhilarating sport only developed beyond the 'piece-of-wood and hope-for-the-best' stage thirty years ago. Then boards were designed specially for Cornish conditions, skin-suits adopted and instructors and lifeguards organised to look after the thousands who wanted to enjoy it.

(*Opposite, bottom*) While the surfers disport themselves below the cliffs, a combine harvester is at work half a mile inland.

Slaughter Bridge (*below*) near Camelford, scene of a battle against the invading Saxons.

(*Opposite*) The long gallery at Llanhydrock House near Bodmin. The main panels of the barrel-vault plaster ceiling depict scenes from the Old Testament. Executed before the Civil War began (1642), it is believed to be the work of the Abbots of Frithelstock near Bideford, known for other spirited work in the region.

(*Opposite*) The setting of the 12th-century castle at Tintagel is everything, the ruins and the traces of an earlier Celtic monastery subordinate to the black cliffs and the encircling sea 200 feet below. The approach across the crumbling isthmus has been made safe for visitors by the Ministry of Works. Archaeological support for the tradition that this was the birthplace of King Arthur is lacking, but no more romantic place for that event could be imagined.

(*Above*) The granite tors of Bodmin Moor are not so numerous as those of Dartmoor (page 35), but make their own impressive contribution to the landscape. These rocks are distinctive with their deep horizontal joints and sharp protrusions, the result of frost acting on the exposed granite.

The rocks of Willapark and Penally Point rear up at the narrow entrance to the tiny, land-locked harbour of Boscastle. For a long time it served as a port for Launceston. Sailing ships were towed in with cargoes of coal or limestone and took on board manganese ore, corn and Delabole slate. The outer breakwater was blown up by a mine during the Second World War and has been rebuilt by the National Trust.

St Anne's Holy Well, Whitstone (*below*), one of the many springs or streams sacred since Celtic times.

Bude Haven (*opposite, top*) was a terminus for Cornwall's only canal before becoming an Edwardian resort.

Lonely Morwenstow church (*opposite, bottom*) stands above the Atlantic cliffs, a ship's figurehead in the churchyard marking the grave of her crew. Parson Hawker, Vicar for forty years, was renowned for his efforts to save or bury the shipwrecked.

Cliffs of the Hartland peninsula, Devon. The rugged grandeur of the Atlantic coast shows in the exposed, contorted layers of sandstones, slates and shales that make up the poorly drained and hard-to-work Culm Measures.

(*Opposite, top*) In Welcombe churchyard a scythe is still handier than a machine.

(*Opposite, bottom*) A local brass band draws people on to the streets of Hartland Town for a celebration.

The narrow cobbled street of Clovelly, broadly stepped in places, falls steeply to the harbour. The ground floors of some cottages are level with the roofs of those below. They were originally built down the side of a stream since diverted. When the sea sparkles in the sunlight it is easy to imagine oneself in Italy.

(*Opposite, top*) Galloway-crossed cattle graze on the wind-swept plateau of the Isle of Lundy. The name means 'Isle of Puffins'. Sadly the numbers of breeding Puffins have declined in recent years but other seabirds and many migrants attract ornithologists.

(*Opposite, bottom*) Hartland Point lighthouse where the Atlantic and the Bristol Channel meet. The flat outline of Lundy, eleven miles away, assists the local weather prophet:

Lundy high, sign of dry.
Lundy plain, sign of rain.
Lundy low, sign of snow.

The town pump at Chulmleigh stands in front of
the old coaching inn, The Kings Arms, converted
to dwellings twenty-five years ago. Horses were
changed here on the long haul over the hills
between Exeter and Barnstaple. The opening of a
new road (1830) and the railway (1854) along the
Taw valley turned hill-top Chulmleigh with its
spacious church, cobbled alleys and many
interesting buildings into the isolated but friendly
village of today.

A striking bow-fronted building faces the Quay at
Bideford, a bustling market town of North Devon.
The inscriptions between the upper windows have
mercifully gone, but this was the former Ship Inn,
now a restaurant, where the lovers of the ill-fated
'Rose of Torridge' formed their Brotherhood in
Westward Ho! Devon-born Charles Kingsley wrote
his long tale of the Elizabethan seadogs in a scarcely
credible spell of less than seven months while
staying at Bideford.

Braunton Burrows (*opposite, top*), a three-mile stretch of dunes north of the Taw/Torridge estuary. They are some of the highest in England rising to 100 feet. About a third of the area is a National Nature Reserve, unique for the botanist. Rarities like the sea pansy and the water germander are common. It is also a stopping place for migrant birds in the autumn.

(*Opposite, bottom*) A mile north of Braunton Burrows, the curving beach of Croyde Bay is a good place for surfing, building sand-castles and exploring rock pools.

On Fridays the 445 foot-long Pannier Market in Barnstaple is crowded with farmer's wives and smallholders selling their produce. The present building was erected in 1854 but Barnstaple has been a market town and the agricultural centre of North Devon for a thousand years. The 17th-century poet and dramatist John Gay, born and educated in the town, would have been familiar with the markets for stock and produce before he went to London, wrote *The Beggar's Opera* and was buried in Westminster Abbey.

Arlington Court, near Barnstaple, the home of the
Chichesters, bequeathed to the National Trust by
Miss Rosalie Caroline Chichester in 1949. The
family furniture in the nursery includes a substantial
rosewood and mahogany cane cot (dated 1820)
which swings on carved pedestals, and a rosewood
whatnot over the fireplace. The pet mice preserved
under glass covers on the mantelshelf are mementos
of Miss Chichester's Victorian childhood.

Cottages, allotments and the village stream at
Swimbridge between South Molton and
Barnstaple. The sporting Parson Jack Russell,
educated at Old Blundell's (page 21) before going
up to Oxford, was Vicar from 1833 to 1880. A man
of unquestioning faith with little regard for books,
he ran his parish better than most country parsons
of his time. Hunting exploits and the breeding of
his famous terriers earned him fame and respect
in a rural society more exuberant than today's.

South Molton is a busy market town of Saxon origin on the river Mole, its rural economy supported by new light industries which have not been allowed to affect the town's character. In Broad Street (*right*) stands the Town Hall with its clock tower, an 18th-century building carried over the pavement and surrounded by other good buildings. The shop at the end of the street with its covered balcony and four Ionic columns is particularly attractive.

(*Below*) A view through the beech copse at Shirwell Cross near Barnstaple looking north-west over the upland pastures where sheep and steers graze on hilly and often marginal land. Sir Francis Chichester's father was Rector of Shirwell and the first single-handed round-the-world yachtsman, a nephew of Miss Chichester of Arlington Court (page 118), spent his youth in this demanding countryside.

The two miles of Woolacombe beach, Morte Bay, are the best sands in North Devon. The dunes and downs between the buildings of Vention on the right and Woolacombe village at the far end of the beach are National Trust property. Behind the village high ground runs out to Morte Point and Morte Stone, grey rocks and reefs of sharp, shining slate that have torn the heart out of many ships.

Ilfracombe is the largest
resort on the North
Devon coast. Lantern
Hill by the harbour is
crowned by the
medieval chapel of
St Nicholas. Its turret
has served as a lighthouse
to mark the harbour
entrance for centuries.
Behind is the massive
rock called the Capstone
which people climb for
a glimpse of Lundy and
the South Wales coast.

Lee Bay, three miles west of Ilfracombe, is a hamlet at the bottom of a thickly wooded combe. It has some old cottages, a profusion of fuchsias and a pub with the unusual and delightful name of The Grampus. The headland to the east with fields pushing out almost to the cliff-edge is Shag Point.

Combe Martin Bay from above Watermouth
Castle, a castellated, Gothick house built about 1825.
Across the bay begin the hump-backed cliffs of the
Exmoor coast: Hangman Point rising to
Little Hangman (744 ft) and behind it
Blackstone Point and the formidable bulk of
Great Hangman (1,004 ft).